10 Habits of Successful People

Achieve Success, Happiness, and Anything You Want!

Blueleo Media

By Lisa j Roberts

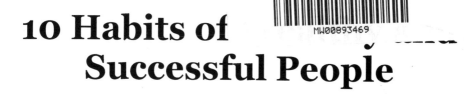

Table of Contents

Introduction

I want to thank you and congratulate you for downloading the book, "10 Habits of Wealthy and successful People - Achieve Success, Happiness, and Anything You Want!"

This book contains proven steps and strategies on how to achieve success and wealth. This is the goal of many people yet only a few have been able to reach it. It should not take a lifetime to achieve success and wealth. Those who use their time and resources wisely and practice the steps and strategies in this book are able to realize their goals sooner rather than later.

Your success relies heavily on your thoughts, actions, and attitudes about life. Within the pages of this book are 10 of the most valuable habits that tap into all three aspects that make you a success. I have outlined how you can apply these habits in your life and how they can benefit your business and your life in general. Make these 10 habits a part of your daily life and see the difference it makes.

Thanks again for downloading this book, I hope you enjoy it!

Chapter 1–Habits of the Wealthy and Successful

Just because you weren't born with a silver spoon in your mouth doesn't mean that you cannot achieve success and amass great wealth. In fact, some of the most successful and wealthiest people in the world were not born rich. Some of them are regular people just like you. But unlike regular individuals, people who become wealthy and successful have a few particular habits that have contributed immensely to their success.

The Importance of Habits in Achieving Success and Wealth

A habit is loosely defined as a behavioral pattern or an action that has been developed over time by repetition or by regularly performing the act. It is a type of action or behavior that a person does without consciously giving it too much thought. An example of a habit could be waking up at precisely 7 o'clock even without setting an alarm. Another example would be smoking a cigarette right after eating. Both of these actions can become habits if done often enough in a person's lifetime.

Habits are important because when you create good habits, you are actually doing things that contribute to your success without expending too much effort or thought. It's like having passive income – you are getting the benefits without doing too much. Habits that promote good health for example will give you energy to do more things that will increase your wealth. Habits that increase your knowledge will enable you to understand how things around you work. This enables you to become innovative and creative, both of which are characteristics of successful and wealthy individuals.

Habits that have become second nature will dictate how you react to certain situations, how you behave in times of adversity, and how you will make your most important decisions in life. Successful people pulled off their accomplishments mostly because of their good habits. This book will tackle 10 of the most important habits of wealthy and successful people. These 10 habits are as follows:

1. Starting the day early and having a morning routine.

2. Always learning and building skills.

3. Setting goals and recording progress.

4. Meditating to relax and focus.

5. Exercising the body and the mind.

6. Getting comfortable with feeling uncomfortable.

7. Think and visualize only winning.

8. Being persistent.

9. Practicing positive self-talk.

10. Taking calculated and planned risks.

Each chapter will be dedicated to one habit to give you a better understanding of that particular habit and how it can benefit you and bring you success. Find out which of these habits you already have and try to develop those that you don't. Having all 10 of them under your belt will do wonders for your mindset and your success.

Chapter 2 – Starting the Day Early and Having a Morning Routine

Think of the first thing that you do in the morning when you wake up. Do you hit the snooze button and go back to sleep? Or do you get up with a smile on your face as soon as the alarm goes off and start getting ready to face the day? If you answered the latter, then could be well on your way to achieving your own success.

It might not sound like a big deal but starting the day early and having a good morning routine are habits that most wealthy and successful people have. Have a look at why these two habits are important and think about how you start your day.

Starting the Day Early

Most regular people set their alarm at night before they go to sleep. They set it at a particular time because they know that waking up at that moment gives them enough time in the morning to get ready and get to work. Some people hit the snooze button for an additional 15 minutes of sleep. This throws off their morning routine. The 15 extra minutes that they spent sleeping would need to be compensated later on by hastening their other morning rituals. The haste adds unnecessary stress and anxiety so early in the morning.

The stress from the morning could be carried over throughout the rest of the day as schedules could get thrown off even with just 15 minutes of extra sleep. People could end up being late for work and missing important meetings. In their haste to leave, they might forget important documents at home. Worse still, they might end up getting into minor accidents because they are driving faster than usual. The possible consequences of hitting the snooze button on the alarm clock are endless.

Unlike other people, a successful person would usually set his alarm at night and then wake up promptly as soon as it goes off. This is his way of controlling his day instead of just reacting to it. When you do your morning routine without the need to hasten your actions, you start the day relaxed and focused. You are not reacting to the idea of being late by rushing through breakfast or skipping it altogether. Instead, you have complete control of your morning and have the peace of mind knowing that you have enough time to do your routine and get to work. When you have complete control over your actions and emotions, you are setting the pace for the rest of your morning routine and the rest of your day as well.

For some people, getting ready means waking up at 5AM, while for others, it could mean waking up at 7AM. That's because some people take longer to get ready while others don't. There's no exact formula for the right time to wake up but most successful people wake up very early in the morning to be able to do more and maximize their day.

Having a Good Morning Routine

How you start your day will dictate how you live your life. If you start your day by answering your emails for example, you are actually doing something for somebody else first thing in the morning. This action tells you that you are prioritizing work over everything else. This could also possibly subconsciously make you think that other people's needs are more important than your own.

On the other hand, if you start by doing personal things like meditating, exercising or setting personal goals for the day, then you are prioritizing yourself before anything else. This is what a successful person does. Successful people know that they have the power to control what happens in their life. Therefore, they make it a priority to work on their selves first thing before everything else. They know that they alone can determine their success or failure so they work on their most important asset which is their own mind, body, heart, and soul.

Start with your body. A good morning routine consists of doing something that will maintain your health. Things like exercising, maintaining proper personal hygiene, eating breakfast, drinking water, and the like are some of the examples of routines that you can do that's good for your body. Having a healthy body gives you more energy to tackle the toughest tasks of your day.

Doing some quiet reading is a good morning routine that will feed your mind. Reading increases your knowledge and feeds the mind. Try quietly reading news articles or try reading a book in the morning and see what happens. Setting personal goals for the day is another way to nourish your mind. Your daily goals give your mind a virtual roadmap that it can follow to help you attain success. Having a clear picture of what you want to achieve could make it easier to reach it. Setting daily goals also helps you organize your day.

For your heart and soul, simple morning routines like cuddling with your loved ones, praying, and meditating can do wonders. Meditation and prayer supports relaxation, whereas spending time with loved ones in the morning promotes bonding and fosters communication. When you feel relaxed, you are more centered and focused at achieving your goals instead of reacting to stress and anxiety. When you feel loved, you feel more inspired to succeed.

Chapter 3 - Always Learning and Building Skills

Probably the most crucial habit of successful and wealthy individuals is the habit of always learning and building on their skills. This particular habit isn't just a habit for success. Learning new things and building on your skills expose you to new experiences and combat boredom. Thus, this is a habit that brings happiness and excitement in your life.

Wealthy and successful people always make it a point to learn something new because they know that new knowledge and new skills mean added value to what they already have. This is also the reason why some companies spend a ton of money on research and development. New knowledge, no matter how small, could potentially double sales and renew interest in a particular product or service.

Take for example a detergent. Notice how every so often companies selling detergent would come up with new and improved versions of their product. They would add fragrance, add bleach cleaning power without fading your clothes, or add fabric conditioner formula to their existing product. They do these because based on their research these are the things that consumers are looking for. The knowledge that they gathered from their research team helped them develop a product or improve on an existing product in order to appeal to the consumers. This action leads to increased sales and increased money in the company's pockets.

Learning something new and building on skills also enable wealthy individuals to innovate. When you know more about how the world works, you become equipped with knowledge on how to fix the problems that the world is facing and make improvements to existing solutions.

The development of transportation is a very good example of this. Back in the day, the only way that people travelled was through walking and riding horses. As people gained more knowledge, they discovered that motorized vehicles can travel greater distances and are faster than horse drawn carriages. Nowadays, all sorts of vehicles are being developed, from hover cars to all-terrain vehicles. Huge engines are replaced by smaller and more efficient machines. Soon you might see flying cars and unmanned vehicles.

The knowledge that man has gained from research and experimentation all contribute to the improvement and innovation that people are experiencing today. Wealthy and successful individuals make it a point to learn new things to remain on top of their game. They innovate and improve their product so that people will want to buy from them over and over.

Learning new things and building your skills will also enable you to do things more efficiently and more effectively. New skills mean improving old, antiquated processes with more efficient and cost effective methods. This means savings for the company in the long run. A good example is the washing machine. Back in the day, people would spend hours in the day manually washing, brushing and cleaning their clothes. This takes up so much time and effort. When news of a machine powered washer came about, people scrambled to purchase these washing machines. Soon people were free to do other things besides washing soiled clothes. They have more time for hobbies and doing things that they enjoy.

Another reason why learning something new and building skills is important to your success is that it makes you more confident. When you know more about a particular topic, you become the go-to person or the subject matter expert on that topic. You also become more confident at dishing out advice, tackling related tasks, and fixing problems related to that topic. People will then trust your opinion and turn to you for help until you are the most sought after and most successful person in that field.

Take a look a successful lawyer. Before becoming successful, a lawyer must continually study the law in order to win his cases. Once he has established himself as a lawyer who always wins, he becomes more in demand and people would want him to represent them. In this case, the success of the lawyer does not depend on things like inherited wealth but rather it depends on his acquired knowledge and skill.

Building skill and learning something new can also keep minds from becoming stagnant and succumbing to brain problems like dementia and Alzheimer's. As you build a skill or learn something new, the brain creates synapses and neurons that help keep a sharp mind and keep it from deteriorating.

The habit of learning something new and building on your skills not only contributes to success but also makes your life more interesting and enjoyable. It is not just a habit for success but also a habit that can improve your life as well. Learning something new can add value to you as a person and to the products that you intend to sell. This creates demand for your products, repeat orders, and loyal customers who can help make your business a success and increase   your   wealth.

Chapter 4 – Setting Goals and Recording Progress

Imagine that you are on a crew member of a ship from the 1920's and are travelling the Atlantic. You and the other seafarers on the ship have been travelling for days and all you see is water, water, and more water. You are unable to see your destination because it is so far away for the naked eye to see. But what keeps you going is the idea that there is land, your destination most likely, somewhere where you can dock, rest, eat, drink and be merry.

In the example above, the destination is the metaphor for your goals, whereas you are represented by the crew member or the ship. Without a goal, or in this case a destination, you will aimlessly roam the vast oceans of the world. Without a goal to guide you, you could get lost, go astray or have a miserable time wandering in the sea.

Goals are made to provide guidance and a sense of purpose. When you have no goals, you could feel lost, despaired, and might even think that your life is totally worthless. You feel like some part of you is missing and that you are merely existing and not really living.

Wealthy and successful people set goals so that they have something to strive for. They set goals to have something to look forward to, to focus on, and to motivate them as they live their daily lives. The sense of purpose makes them more excited to get up in the morning and go to work. It keeps their mind sharp, their bodies active, and their attitudes positive to have something to look forward to everyday.

When wealthy and successful people set goals they make sure to set S.M.A.R.T. goals:

1. **S**pecific – Goals have to be specific otherwise it will be hard to attain. Compare these two goals and see which ones seem easier to achieve.

   For instance: a 50% increase in sales by the end of the year VS having more customers liking the product

   The former gives you a specific target that you have to hit while the latter gives a vague description of what you want to have. The ambiguity of the second goal makes it harder for you to picture what it is that you want to achieve. The goal is also uncertain as there is no way to know whether the customers are indeed liking or not liking the product.

2. **M**easurable – A goal has to be measurable otherwise you will not know if you are succeeding or if you are failing. Taking the example above, the increase in sales can be measured by the sales figures at the end of the day and can be tallied until the end of the year to be compared with last year's figures. "Having more customers like the product," on the other hand, may be measurable using a customer satisfaction survey but could still yield inconclusive results versus the more specific goal.

   In measuring your goal, you are also able to track your progress. When you have tangible numbers and data to back up your goals, it is easy to see how far or how near you are from achieving it. If you are still behind, you can try to implement processes to boost your sales and achieve your goals. If you are right on track, then you can rest easy knowing that everything is going as planned.

3. **A**ttainable – It is perfectly alright to dream of owning a yacht, an expensive sports car, a helicopter, and your own private island somewhere in the Pacific. These are great goals to strive for, but your goals should be something that's entirely possible at a certain moment in your life. If you are

just starting out, with no means and no talent to help make your dreams come true, then it might be better to set a smaller and achievable goal using the things you have at the moment.

When you set attainable goals and you are able to achieve them, you get a boost of confidence and become more motivated to get to a higher level of goal setting. Simple goals at the beginning can also become stepping stones for bigger goals later on in life.

4. **R**elevant – Relevant goals are goals that you set to solve your most pressing problems. You should have goals that meet your needs and not other people's. Relevant goals should mean something to you and not just a passing phase in your life. It should also be something that you can take action on and have the means to achieve.

   An example of a relevant goal is for a student is to get a score of B+ or higher in the final exam in order to avoid retaking chemistry next semester. In business, an example of a relevant goal could be to increase sales by 100% until the end of the year for a particular product so that it won't be shelved or retired.

5. **T**imely – Similar to relevant goals, timely goals solve the most current problems that you are facing and should meet a current need that you want to achieve. It should also be something that you can achieve in the near future.

   An example of a timely goal is when you try to strike while the iron is hot. You know that there is a high demand for lip kits, for example. In order to take advantage of this demand, you set a goal of creating and selling 30 lip kits per day. If there is no demand for lip kits, then this goal isn't timely.

Remember to make goals that fit your current need and capacity, otherwise you'll feel like these goals are impossible to meet. It is better to start with smaller goals and work your way up to bigger goals once you have the means to achieve them.

Chapter 5 - Meditation to Relax and Focus

Meditation takes little effort but can have a huge impact on your success. Meditation is a way to train your mind to delve deeper inward (towards yourself or your subconscious) or outward (towards your surroundings or the universe in general) depending on what it is that you need. It is a way to induce an altered state of consciousness that lets your mind "travel" without you moving.

There are different types of meditation techniques that successful and wealthy individuals use. Some of them are done to promote relaxation which can be very helpful during stressful periods. As you go about your day, you may encounter stressful situations that could put your mind out of focus and make you anxious. You may be faced with adversities, tough decisions, and distractions that keep you from achieving your goals. When you meditate, you clear your mind from all of these external distractions and overload of information so that you can relax and bring your focus back to the things that are important.

Many successful and wealthy individuals practice meditation in order to become more mindful of their thoughts and actions. This type of meditation technique helps develop self-awareness. When you are mindful of your thoughts and actions, you become better at handling difficult situations and become less likely to put the wrong foot forward. Developing self-awareness can also mean getting in touch with your inner self. Within each person is an inner self that could be considered as a more intuitive and more centered version of you. When you meditate, you quiet your mind so that you can tap into that version of yourself and make better decisions that could affect your success.

Meditation also promotes a sense of well-being and promotes good health. It helps lower your risk of developing cardiovascular diseases and improves your immune system by helping you relax. Breathing techniques used in meditation can help lower your blood pressure and lower your heart rate as well. When this happens, you become healthier and you would have increased your life span.

Meditation also improves concentration and helps you focus even if there are so many distracting things around you. When you are faced with feelings of self-doubt, anxiety, desolation, and hopelessness meditation can help bring back your focus from the negative aspects of your life back to the good things that make your life meaningful and enjoyable. When you are free of negative and unnecessary thoughts, your mind becomes free to take in important information and have a more positive outlook towards life. You also become free of feelings that keep you from succeeding.

Another great thing about meditation is that it lessens (and often helps eliminate) fear and anger. When you let feelings of fear go, you are more open to accepting challenges and changes in your life. You become more courageous and more likely to take risks that could possibly bring your success. Meditation keeps anger away from your thoughts and heart by helping you accept the things you cannot change and let go of your ill feelings whenever things don't go your way.

Meditation makes you more tolerant of other people so that you won't feel angry over little mistakes that other people do. It also calms you down so that even when all you want to do is scream and shout at somebody, you are better at keeping your anger at bay and won't end up regretting the things you have said or done later on. When you let go of fear and anger, you sleep better at night and are less likely to have enemies.

Meditation can benefit not just your success but your overall wellness. It is a great way to wind yourself down after a hectic day so that you can reflect on the things that did wrong and the things that you did right. Knowing these things can help you make better decisions tomorrow. You should make it a point to practice meditation and to make it part of your daily routine.

Chapter 6 - Exercising the Body and the Mind

Having a healthy mind and body lets you do more with your time and gives you more energy to do the things that will help you succeed. If that isn't motivation enough to make a habit out of exercising both your mind and body, then maybe this will:

Being healthy in both mind and body lets you enjoy the fruits of your success longer by making you healthy enough create more memories, spend your money, and experience the best of what the world has to offer. It also helps you have more meaningful relationships and spend quality time with your loved ones. A healthy mind and body can also make you more attractive to the people you want to partner with romantically and professionally.

Here are other benefits of exercising the body and the mind to motivate you even more:

Body

1. You don't get sick often – Exercise keeps you healthy, lowers your cholesterol, and strengthens your immune system. When you exercise, you are making your muscles stronger and more flexible so you won't get muscle related injuries. Increased physical activity keeps your heart pumping and lowers the bad cholesterol in the body.

2. You live longer – It's no secret that one of the leading causes of some of the deadliest health problems like diabetes, cancer, and heart attack is obesity. Exercising helps you eliminate unwanted fat that could cause these life threatening diseases.

3. You'll look great and your self-esteem will improve – Looking your best makes you feel good about yourself and increases your confidence. When you exercise, you are increasing muscle and reducing fat. This makes your clothes fit better and makes it easier for you to move around. You won't feel winded easily after just one flight of stairs or you won't feel shy about walking around the beach in your bathing suit.

4. You'll feel happy – When you exercise, you release feel good hormones called endorphins. This makes you less likely to feel depressed or unhappy. When you exercise in the morning for example, these endorphins put you in a good mood which can carry over throughout your day.

5. You'll have more energy – Some people think that exercising makes you feel tired. The answer is yes and no. Yes, you will feel tired while you are exercising because you are exerting effort. Later on, when you have rested after your exercise, you'll feel energized and you will be able to breeze through your tasks better and more efficient than if you didn't exercise.

Mind

1. You start thinking out of the box – Most successful and wealthy people are out of the box thinkers. They see problems from different angles and provide solutions that some people never even consider as possible. When you exercise your mind, you become more open to out of the box ideas that could later on become the ticket to your instant success.

2. You become more open to change – Successful people understand that in order to move forward, things must

change. When you train your mind to become more receptive to change, then you can adapt better and not be held back by antiquated beliefs that may no longer apply to the vast changing world.

3. You make quick and calculated decisions easily – Opportunities for success sometimes come at the most inappropriate moments. When your mind is at its sharpest you become better at making decisions even when faced with difficult choices.

4. You'll be able to concentrate better and work smarter – A sharp mind can see gaps and problem areas that can be improved. This can make you work more effectively and efficiently than others which could pave the way to your success.

5. You become more creative – Creativity is a trait that all successful individuals have. This doesn't mean that you have to be good at drawing or painting. Being creative can mean being good at creating solutions, being inventive or good at innovating.

Having sound mind and body is not an impossible feat no matter what your situation in life is. There are plenty of exercise routines that don't require expensive gym equipment so there's no excuse for you not to exercise. The more you do it the more it becomes a habit and comes to your naturally like second nature.

Try exercising consistently for an entire month at the same time every day and see what happens. Exercise your mind regularly by reading, playing games that keep the mind sharp, and doing things that get you out of your comfort zone. The more you challenge your brain the better it becomes at solving problems and creating innovative ideas. Do exercises that enrich your mind and body regularly and before you know it you'll soon be able to achieve the success   and   gain   wealth.

Chapter 7 - Getting Comfortable with Feeling Uncomfortable

In your lifetime, you'll encounter difficulties and challenges that push you to your limit. Most people try to wade through life and avoid conflicts and hardships as much as possible. Other, more successful individuals don't try to avoid it and instead do their best to get comfortable with it.

When you are comfortable when faced with an uncomfortable situation, you become grace under pressure personified. You are that person who looks calm and has his thoughts collected while everybody else is panicking. Take for example in a courtroom. The lawyer who never loses his cool is usually the one who has prepared well for the case and has more experience than the other lawyer. He is comfortable in a situation that would usually faze a lawyer who just graduated from law school.

Here are other examples of common uncomfortable situations and how you should handle them:

Meeting a person who is more famous, more influential, or more powerful than you is a situation that is exciting but could also be very uncomfortable. But it is something that you do because it is a great opportunity to be seen with this important person. You also do it because the ties that will be forged during this meeting could later on open doors for you or your business. That's the exciting part. What makes it uncomfortable is when you feel afraid that you will say or do something wrong which can put you in the person's bad graces and lose all the good opportunities that come with that meeting. The more you stress about it, the more likely you are to commit the faux pas that you dread. So what should you do?

To become comfortable in this situation, you must try to think of the meeting as something that's not a big deal. Treat the other person like you would treat a good friend or a revered mentor. Also, try to keep in mind all your accomplishments and the success that you have achieved. This will put things in perspective as you realize that you too are worth knowing and that they are should be just as honored to know someone like you.

Another type of uncomfortable situation that you could encounter is when you are being bullied or being harassed. Nobody wants to be bullied and successful people are never victims of bullying and harassment. When faced with a hostile situation like this, successful people stand up for themselves and don't back down. When you stand up for yourself, you don't give your opponent power to make you feel like a weakling and a victim. You will be the known as the one who doesn't back down and the one who projects an image of bravery which can later on inspire others to fight and not be a victim too.

Uncomfortable situations range from mildly uncomfortable (as in the case of giving talks to a roomful of strangers) to extremely uncomfortable (as in the case of being bullied or harassed). What sets successful people apart is how they feel in these situations. Successful people try their best not to feel stressed or anxious during these uncomfortable moments in their careers. They train themselves to be calm and level headed despite the stressful situation so that they can still make good decisions and not act on impulse. When you feel comfortable in stressful situations, you become less likely to make mistakes and do things that you might regret later on.

It's not an easy thing to do to be calm while the world outside is full of problems and chaos. One trick that can help you be comfortable in an uncomfortable situation is to take deep breaths. Focusing on your deep breaths calms you down and slows your heartbeat. When you are feeling nervous or stressed it helps to focus on other things besides your problems.

Another trick you can apply to make an uncomfortable situation more bearable is to think of the rewards that come after the ordeal is over. You can go for margaritas after a particularly grueling meeting or you can take a weeklong vacation to make up for all those overtime hours you've put in just to meet a very tight deadline. When you have something to look forward to, your burden will feel less difficult even for just a little bit.

The most important trick that can make being comfortable in uncomfortable situations into a habit is to practice. Face uncomfortable situations with success in mind. Think of positive outcomes instead of focusing on what could go wrong. The more you train yourself to be alright even when there are problems around, the more comfortable you will feel when faced with an uncomfortable situation in the future. Don't be too hard on yourself if you slip and start stressing. Try to calm yourself down and try again.

Chapter 8 - Think and Visualize Only Winning

Mood boards and online picture boards are popular with people who work in visual merchandizing and creative professions like fashion design and interior decoration. They use it to piece together "puzzles" that could make their next clothing line whole or to create a vision board for the design of a client's interior. This vision board allows them to see the entire picture before they set it in production. This also gives their clients a peek at what goes on in their creative mind before they translate these creations in real life.

Similar to a designer's vision board when you have a clear picture of what it looks like to win, to be successful, and to achieve something, be it an actual visual representation or a virtual picture in your head, you are actually ingraining in your subconscious that this is the thing that you need to strive for. You are visually giving your brain a picture of what it is you want to achieve. Your brain, being the good brain that it is, will somehow make things happen.

Some new age practitioners likened this phenomenon to what is called the law of attraction. The premise of the law of attraction is that when you place your focus on something you desire, you will somehow attract it and it will have an impact in your life. When you think of something good, you will attract good. When you think of something bad, you will attract bad things.

Similarly, when you picture in your head something you want to achieve or that you are winning at something, you are sending a message out to the universe that this is what you want in your life. And eventually, by some cosmic power, the universe conspires to make it happen.

Even if it doesn't have something to do with laws of attraction, making a habit of thinking and visualizing yourself as a winner and a success will have a positive effect on your life. Visualizing your goals gives your brain a clear picture of what it needs to achieve. A clear vision of your goals can serve as a light at the end of a dark tunnel when you sometimes feel lost and inadequate.

Aside from creating mood boards and vision boards, here are some other great examples of techniques that can help you realize your goals:

1. Putting a physical reminder of what it is that you want to achieve – get that tiny polka dot bikini out from inside your closet to help you get motivated to workout. Put your bikini on display where you can easily see it so that you are reminded everyday of what you want to achieve. Put it right in front of your bed so that you'll have something to motivate you when you don't feel like exercising.

2. Look at the lives of successful people – having someone to emulate can make visualizing what success looks like easier. Just make sure that you don't try to copy other people's lives entirely. Take a few cues from the lives of successful people and people you admire and work from there.

3. Keep repeating that vision in your head over and over – think about winning first immediately when you wake up in the morning and make it a point to visualize it over and over in your head often throughout the day. Let it be your last thought before you go to sleep as well. It sometimes helps to close your eyes as you picture it in your head.

4. Tell yourself that "you can do this" – be your own cheerleader and tell yourself that you can do this. Believe

in your abilities and be confident. Motivate yourself by looking at your talents and telling yourself that these are good enough to merit that win.

5. Create a tunnel vision – Notice how horses have blinders or blinkers to keep them from being distracted by their surroundings. These blinders help them focus on the finish line and not get sidetracked by the other horses racing with them. If you want to get that beach body, for example, keep your focus on your diet by avoiding visual temptation. Stop looking at food networks and cooking channels. When dining out, ignore other people's food and focus on your salad. It will be tough but will be totally worth it when you achieve your ideal weight.

When you think about winning, remember to still keep your morals and manners in place. Some people focus solely on winning that they don't care who they step on as long as they get what they want. Be aware of your actions and don't let competition get the best of you. Winning matters but maintaining a good reputation and having friends you can trust as you succeed in life are precious blessings that not everyone has.

Chapter 9 - Persistence is the key

A lot of wealthy and successful people say that the road to success is never easy. It often requires sacrifice, sweat, blood and tears in order for you to achieve your goals and enjoy a successful life. On top of all that, you will encounter mistakes, failures and rejections along the way. All these can easily discourage and distract you from achieving your goals. What keeps successful people from throwing in the towel is their persistence.

Persistence means that you never give up on working and achieving your goals despite all the hardships and obstacles that you encounter along the way. It is so easy to up and quit when you are faced with tough and seemingly impossible to overcome obstacles. But when you persist and never give up, there is deeper feeling of satisfaction in knowing that you worked through it and then end up winning.

Take Jack Ma for example. The founder of a multi-million dollar online buy and sell company was said to have been rejected by Harvard 10 times before he finally succeeded in life. Other famous success stories include Thomas Edison who was described by his teachers as someone who is "too stupid to learn anything" and Walt Disney who was once fired from a job at a newspaper company because he supposedly "lacked imagination". Today, Thomas Edison has over 1,000 patents to his name and is a world famous inventor. Walt Disney's company is now worth billions of dollars and is the one place where imagination thrives. These setbacks obviously did not deter them from pursuing their dreams and they have succeeded.

These people, who are now millionaires and billionaires in their own rights, became successful because they believed in their talents.

They know that the opinion of one person is not the opinion of the entire planet. They believe that somewhere in the world there is a person who share their ideals and could help them succeed. They persisted with their passion, whether it's for drawing or for inventing, without heeding the naysayers who always try to bring them down.

Persistent people succeed in life because they don't see mistakes and failures as permanent roadblocks to their success. They see them as temporary setbacks where lessons can be learned. Mistakes are opportunities to try again and not quit altogether. It just means they haven't found the right formula yet so they need to start again. Their positive attitude towards failure help keep them going and trying another experiment using different variables from their previous failed experiments.

Being persistent is considered as a quality of a person with a strong character and inner strength. A person who is persistent will endure the hardships and take on the toughest of tasks in order to gain more rewards. They are the ones who never complain and never quit. Making a habit out of persistence can make you a winner no matter what the outcome is. Only people who persist are able to reach their dreams.

Don't confuse persistence with being a pest. The paparazzi are perfect examples of what being a pest is. To them, it's just being persistent when they pursue a celebrity for a picture. But when they are trying to get photos of a celebrity's private or intimate moments, then it's no longer persistence. There have also been many instances where people get into accidents just by trying to avoid paparazzi. There's a fine line between persistence and being a pest. Don't be the latter.

To make a habit of being persistent you must practice strengthening your willpower. You must also discipline yourself into enduring despite all the hardships that come your way. Setbacks are already considered as a given. You just have to power through it and try again.

If your business venture did not work out, don't be discouraged. Learn from your mistakes, look at it from a different angle and try again. Even if you get rejected several times, don't let it dampen your spirits. Thomas Edison was once said that for his many failed experiment he insisted that he did not fail and that he just found 10,000 ways that did not work. Look at the positive side of failure and learn from it.

Find people whom you trust and love to help you get up from this setback. Take a breather and then try again. Sooner or later you will find something that will succeed. It's just a matter of finding the right formula at the right moment. Re-evaluate, review and try again. Sometimes all it takes is one tiny adjustment to make a difference between succeeding and failing.

Whether you like it or not, at some point in your life, you will encounter failures and mistakes. How you handle these problems dictates how much you will succeed in life. Handle problems like they are insurmountable obstacles and you would have stopped experimenting altogether and never experience success. But handle them as temporary setbacks and lessons learned and you would have been able to reach the right formula for success with your persistence.

Chapter 10 - Practicing Positive Self-talk

Look at yourself in the mirror and think about what you see. Do you see a beautiful person who's got so much potential for success? Or do you see someone who looks haggard, depressing and hopeless? If you see the latter then it's time to rethink about your opinion of yourself. It's time to change your thoughts from negative to positive.

Wealthy and successful people know that the power of positive self-talk is instrumental to their success. They know that the more they believe in their abilities, the more they will succeed. When they believe that they have the ability to make mountains move, then their actions get inspired by their thoughts.

To get into the habit of practicing positive self-talk you should try to do the following:

1. Get rid of all the negative thoughts – Do you mentally berate yourself every time you do something wrong? Do you think less of yourself when you look at fashion magazines and you don't look like any of the models featured there? Stop all these negative thoughts at once. These don't do you and your self-esteem any good.

   Think instead of things that you like about yourself. Look at the beauty within you and keep that on top of your mind. Notice how kind and patient you are with animals or how pretty you look when you smile. Be self-aware and really think hard about what makes you someone worth knowing.

   Some people find this hard to do especially if they've been told throughout their lifetime that they are not good enough or they don't have what it takes. For example, if you've been with an abusive partner for a long time who likes to control you by telling you that you are fat and ugly then it might take some time to condition your thoughts from negative to positive. It might take a while but it is entirely possible.

2. Remove the words "I can't" from your vocabulary – When faced with difficulties you sometimes think that it is too hard to go on and that you can't do it. Stop thinking like that. When you tell yourself at the beginning that you can't then you already failed even before you started. Replace thoughts of "I can't" with thoughts of "I'll try". 100% of the time, people who try are the ones who eventually succeed. Don't knock yourself out before you even get started.

   Remove self-limiting thoughts from your mind. Remove words like "this is impossible" or "this is hopeless". The more you tell yourself this, the more you will believe it. You won't succeed with a defeatist attitude.

3. Start with positive thoughts first thing in the morning – Your life could be overwhelming at times. You get so busy that you never have a moment to give yourself a good positive self-talk. To get your daily dose, why not try doing it first thing in the morning. As soon as you wake up, tell yourself that you are going to do great things today, that you are a wonderful, kind and successful person, and that there's nothing that can make you think otherwise. Make it a part of your morning routine to tell yourself that you are a good person. Include it in your daily meditation to think of the great things that you do. When you are lying down on your bed, you can also try mentally listing down the positive things about you starting from the tips of your toes to the ends of your hair.

4. Use the walls of your home for positive reinforcement – Put up positive slogans, signs and pictures that promote

success and happiness. This is a helpful exercise for people who are struggling to find the positive things in their life. Having a visual representation that you can see often will remind you of how great you are. Put up happy pictures of you and your loved ones to inspire you to be happy throughout the day. You can even buy inexpensive wall art that could instill self-affirming thoughts in you.

5. Surround yourself with people who are supportive of you and your cause – being around negative people can rub off on you easily. Don't be afraid to edit people from your life. If you feel like someone is being overly negative and zapping all your positivity away, then limit spending time with them as much as possible. They'll be the ones to pull you down from your success so get rid of them.

6. Repetition and practice is the key – No matter how ridiculous or self -serving you think it sounds, just keep thinking of positive thoughts about yourself. Repeat them until they stick to your subconscious. Read positive thoughts aloud and make a mantra out of them. Repeat your mantra until you start to believe it.

7. Think happy thoughts – Your thoughts will dictate your actions so always think of happy thoughts. Look at the silver lining in every situation no matter how awful it may seem. See the good in people and do not judge them immediately for one mistake that they have committed. Reflect on instances that make you happy and keep those thoughts in mind whenever you feel down. Keep trying and you'll soon get the hand of positive self-talk.

Chapter 11 - Taking calculated and planned risks

Most successful entrepreneurs are risk takers both in life and in business. They understand that in order to succeed, they have to take steps that are potentially life altering in order to reap huge rewards. But don't think that they are foolish enough to gamble everything away by taking dangerous risks. What they do is to take calculated and planned risks that won't put their business in jeopardy and could help them make a ton of money in the process.

A bad risk sometimes results from thoughtlessness and impulsive actions. These usually end up making you lose more money instead of the opposite. An example of a bad risk is doing an illegal thing just to save more money or cutting corners that could potentially endanger other people's lives just to make a bigger profit.

Calculated and planned risks on the other hand are risks that need careful analysis and planning. When you take calculated risks, you would normally require some background information, historical data, and statistical analysis before you make your next move. These kinds of information will give you an insight on people's buying patterns, potential gains and losses and profit projections to help you make your decision.

When you take calculated risk, remember to strike a balance between everyday work and the risk that you are taking. Don't put all your eggs in one basket. In this case, don't put all your money on going after a risky venture. Instead, maintain the parts of your business that are making profit while taking that calculated risk to move your company forward.

Don't go for every opportunity that presents itself to you. Study each one carefully before making a decision. You don't want to be in over your head in debt because you tried to grab all the opportunities at the same time. Evaluate which ones are worth doing now and which ones can be done later.

One of the riskiest parts of doing business is expanding operations. There are so many factors that can affect expansion that companies are sometimes hesitant to do it. One such factor could be that the surge of the demand for your product may wane quickly before you even got a chance to finish expansion. It is risky because you might not be able to sustain the costs that you can incur with maintaining this expansion and end up losing more. To make a calculated risk regarding expansion, companies would study, take customer surveys and rely on statistical data in order to back up the need for an expansion.

Another risky venture is developing a new product. In order to grow your company, you must be willing to adapt to the changing world. A new product is sometimes needed in order to increase sales and interest in your company. It is risky because a new product might not be as well received as your other products. If this happens, you would have expended a lot of time, money, and effort on something that people didn't pick up on. But you still do it because as an entrepreneur, this is one of the best ways to move your company forward. To make a calculated risk of creating a new product, you must take on market research and be ready for feedback that's both positive and negative. Positive feedback will let you know which ones you are doing right and negative feedback will help you fix what it is that you did wrong. Either way, you get valuable information.

Some people will discourage you from taking that risk. Some of them have good intentions and are just afraid that you might fail.

Others are just manipulative because they want the opportunity for themselves. When faced with advice from other people, try to listen to what your gut is telling you. Your intuition will warn you if there is danger so you should always listen to it. Meditate and be silent as you listen to what your inner self is telling you before you make your decision. Sometimes the best advice comes from within you.

Risks will always be a part of life. In order to make huge gains, you must be willing to take calculated and planned risks. Don't be afraid to take a leap but make sure that you have the data, the resources, and the strength to face what lies ahead. You might not always get what you planned but you will never know success if you didn't try at all. Take a risk but be smart about it. Decide based on valid supporting data and not just on impulse. Trust your gut, trust your team, and trust yourself to make the right move towards your success.

Conclusion

Thank you again for downloading this book!

I hope this book was able to help you know more about the 10 habits of successful individuals and have inspired you to take action towards your own success.

The next step is to apply what you have learned in this book. Until you fully apply what you have learned, the information does not have power. World renowned speaker and best-selling author, Ricky Baldasso often says 'Knowledge is not enough. You must take action!' It is not through acquiring new information that the quality of our lives improves, but through taking new actions, so I encourage you from the bottom of my heart to take action on what you have learned here and believe me, the only problem you'll have is that you didn't read this book 6 months ago and take action then!

Finally, if you enjoyed this book, please take the time to share your thoughts and post a review on Amazon. It'd be greatly appreciated!

Thank you and good luck!

Lisa j Roberts

Made in the USA
Columbia, SC
27 July 2018